Going to School

Written by Rebecca Jane Smith
Illustrated by Lyn Kriegler

My big brother was sick today.
I had to walk to the bus
all by myself.

"Here's your lunch,"
said Mum.
"Hurry, or you'll miss the bus.
Don't forget to shut the gates,"
she said.

"No, Mum, I won't forget to shut the gates. Goodbye."

“Sorry, Kitty,
I can’t play with you now.
I’m catching the bus
by myself today.”

"Hello, Scamp. I can't stop.
I'm catching the bus
by myself today."

“Go back, Curly,
you can’t come with me.
I’m catching the bus
by myself today.”

“Oh, no, Molly,
I don’t have time
to milk you now.
I’m catching the bus
by myself today.”

"Sorry, little ducks!
No food for you now.
I will bring you some
after school.
I'm catching the bus
by myself today."

“Hello, Dusty.
I can’t stop
to give you a pat.
I have to hurry.
I’m catching the bus
by myself today.”

“Oh, no! The bus is here!
I’d better run.”

"Hello, Mrs Sharp.
Thanks for waiting.
I'm catching the bus
by myself today!"